IDEAS IN F

Narcissism

Jeremy Holmes

Series editor: Ivan Ward

ICON BOOKS UK

TOTEM BOOKS USA

Published in the UK in 2001
by Icon Books Ltd., Grange Road,
Duxford, Cambridge CB2 4QF
E-mail: info@iconbooks.co.uk
www.iconbooks.co.uk

Published in the USA in 2001
by Totem Books
Inquiries to: Icon Books Ltd.,
Grange Road, Duxford,
Cambridge CB2 4QF, UK

Sold in the UK, Europe, South Africa
and Asia by Faber and Faber Ltd.,
3 Queen Square, London WC1N 3AU
or their agents

Distributed to the trade in the USA
by National Book Network Inc.,
4720 Boston Way, Lanham,
Maryland 20706

Distributed in the UK, Europe,
South Africa and Asia by
Macmillan Distribution Ltd.,
Houndmills, Basingstoke RG21 6XS

Distributed in Canada by
Penguin Books Canada,
10 Alcorn Avenue, Suite 300,
Toronto, Ontario M4V 3B2

Published in Australia in 2001
by Allen & Unwin Pty. Ltd.,
PO Box 8500, 83 Alexander Street,
Crows Nest, NSW 2065

ISBN 1 84046 245 0

Text copyright © 2001 Jeremy Holmes

The author has asserted his moral rights.

Series editor: Ivan Ward

No part of this book may be reproduced in any form, or by any
means, without prior permission in writing from the publisher.

Typesetting by Hands Fotoset

Printed and bound in the UK by
Cox & Wyman Ltd., Reading

Introduction

Narcissism starts from mirrors – from the mirroring mother, whose gleaming eye and responsive smile reflects delight in her child, through the seductive yet claustrophobic 'hall of mirrors' of overprotective parents, the suicidal patient confronting the cold lifeless mirror of the empty bathroom, to the watery surface that shatters into a thousand pieces as Narcissus vainly reaches out to embrace his own reflection.

We are all fascinated by mirrors. But who and what do we behold when we peer into them? Does what we see seem alien – a stranger whom we hardly recognise? Do we look 'alright' – do we say to ourselves 'you'll do' as we make ready for a party? Do we secretly admire what we see, or collapse in horror and loathing like the fairy-tale dwarf seeing his deformity for the first time? Do we preen ourselves in front of the mirror, pirouetting with backwards glance, flirting with our own image? Or do we, like Rembrandt, gaze squarely at the face that stares back at us, trying with every fibre to penetrate the mysteries of the self – a self that is at once so familiar and so strange?

Havelock Ellis, the late 19th-century sexologist, was the first to link the classical Narcissus myth with psychological difficulty, seeing homosexuality, then regarded as a sexual perversion, as a pathology of self-love; a man loves another man, a woman a woman, who is like (a reflection of) him or herself, rather than the supposedly appropriate opposing gender. Hence the Oxford English Dictionary definition of narcissism, a term coined by Wilhelm Nacke in reviewing Ellis' work, as 'morbid self-love or self-admiration'. Note the necessary qualifier, 'morbid' – self-love is not necessarily problematic, and indeed is generally seen as a mark of psychological health.

The term 'narcissism' can be used in a number of distinct ways. In a *lay* sense it tends to be synonymous with *self-centredness* or *self-preoccupation*, and is appropriately used in describing people whose speech is littered with the pronoun 'I'; whose conversation tends to take the form of what one long-suffering spouse of a chronic narcissist dubbed 'Radio Me'. For Charles Rycroft, narcissism is a variant of:

solipsism . . . the tendency to use oneself as the point of reference round which experience is organised. In this sense the discovery that one is not the only pebble on the beach and that the world was not constructed solely for one's own benefit involves a loss of narcissism.[1]

There is an implicit value judgement here which, as we shall see, psychoanalysis tries to theorise: to be self-centred is normal and acceptable in the young, but, if 'selfishness' persists into adult life, it is maladaptive and liable to be frowned upon. Here consideration for others and altruism are contrasted with the inability or refusal to see the world from anything other than one's own point of view, with consequent potential for trampling on other's feelings.

The idea of narcissism has been used *sociologically* by authors such as Christopher Lasch to describe a constellation of attitudes characterised by extreme individualism, lack of interest in the past or future, disregard for others, preoccupation with personal relationships at the expense of political activity, and lack of concern about social cohesion.[2] People so described (no doubt not without a streak of puritanical envy) might be the 'me generation' of today's young affluent middle class, or the decadent and *fin de siècle* hedonists of the late 19th-century European upper classes, so beautifully depicted by Oscar Wilde (of whom more below). Collective or group narcissism underlies such diverse phenomena as delusions of racial superiority, and various cults and messianic groupings in which individual narcissism may be either legitimised or submerged in devotion to a charismatic leader.

Psychoanalytic ideas about narcissism fall under three distinct headings: libidinal narcissism, destructive narcissism, and healthy narcissism. Sigmund Freud saw 'primary narcissism' as a normal developmental stage in which the infant thinks only, and blissfully, of itself. This is a precursor of *object relations*, the capacity to relate to – 'invest libido in' – others. Freud believed that people suffering from paranoia and schizophrenia, and to some extent hypochondriacal illnesses, regressed, often in the face of loss, to a 'secondary' narcissistic state in which 'libido' (here conceptualised as a kind of psychic fluid) is withdrawn from the external world and reinvested in themselves and their own bodies. Ronald Britton calls this state of psychic withdrawal into the self 'libidinal narcissism'.[3]

By contrast, Karl Abraham, and later the Kleinian school (especially Herbert Rosenfeld and Otto Kernberg), emphasise the destructive aspects of narcissism, in which the narcissist pathologically envies, hates, and actively seeks to destroy the object, that is *the other*. Only the self can be allowed to exist. Herbert Rosenfeld uses the powerful metaphor of the 'mafia gang' which is imagined taking over the mind, ruthlessly insisting that no external relationship is permissible. This triumphant 'thick-skinned' narcissism is contrasted with 'thin-skinned' libidinal narcissism, which is more defensive than destructive.[4]

A third psychoanalytic approach to narcissism is associated with the self-psychology school of Heinz Kohut.[5] Kohut saw narcissism, i.e. self-love, and object-love not as lying on a continuum, but as two distinct developmental lines which persist throughout life, each with its own characteristic features and pathologies. He emphasised the healthy aspect of narcissism, seeing such phenomena as parental adoration of their children, the child's excitement in itself and its world, and 'normal' hopes, aspirations, ambitions and ideals as all belonging to the sphere of positive narcissism. In this model, as development proceeds, narcissism is not replaced by object-love but, rather, is tempered by gradual disillusionment so that in maturity it continues to underlie good self-esteem and *realistic* goals. 'Secondary narcissism', and the inability to progress along the path of moderated self-love, result from 'narcissistic wounds', often arising out of parental neglect or abuse. Here, lacking external validation of their narcissism ('*We* do not find you loveable'), individuals fall back on self-love so that at least a modicum of hope and motivation may survive.

Many of these psychoanalytic ideas are brought together in the psychiatric sense of narcissism contained in Kernberg's notion of 'narcissistic personality disorder', in which the sufferer is self-centred and demanding, overestimates his or her own abilities and specialness, is envious, exploitative and unable to consider others' feelings – but underneath this bombastic self-importance, the sufferer is often deeply depressed and has profound feelings of emptiness. As we shall see, finding ways to help these individuals is a major challenge for psychotherapy.

Clinical Manifestations of Narcissism

In this section I shall consider aspects of narcissism as they might arise in a psychoanalytic situation, which I divide, somewhat artificially, into 'necessary narcissism', everyday 'clinical narcissism', and 'entrenched narcissism'.

The most obvious example of necessary narcissism

is to be found in normal parental fascination and pride in their children, which, as we shall see, is a prerequisite if children are to develop good self-esteem. As Freud puts it:

Parental love, which is so moving and at bottom so childish, is nothing but parent's narcissism born again, which, transformed into object-love, unmistakably reveals its former nature.[6]

Of course, most parents are able to temper their narcissistic over-investment with realism. They can also see their offspring as separate beings, with their own projects, whose purpose is not merely to fulfil their parents' hopes and ambitions. Also, as Neville Symmington points out, effective parenting involves a huge sacrifice of narcissism, putting aside one's own self-centredness in order to concentrate on one's child, and allowing that child access to one's partner.

There are, however, those individuals who cannot *not* talk about their children, especially if successful, thereby inducing a certain envy and weariness in the listener. Similarly, those whose conversation consists mainly of boasting about their own achievements, wealth, and the important and powerful people with whom they are connected, are often compensating for feelings of insignificance and inferiority. Their conversation is peppered with the pronouns 'I' and 'me' and 'mine'; their primary need is to be centre stage, yet with little apparent interest in the lives and reactions of their audience. They may be entertaining and fascinating, or sometimes unbearable bores.

Again, they may excite envy, since most of us have a well of residual narcissism which our developmental process has helped keep in check, but which is never fully abandoned, only partially transcended in favour of the more palpable satisfactions of object relationships. The rich and famous, and their attendant publicity machines, provide necessary icons into which the majority of us who lead mundane lives can project our own secret narcissistic hopes and desires. The 'narcissistic bubble' with its brilliant reflections floats tantalisingly above our heads; when it bursts, the occupant is left naked and pitifully vulnerable.

The therapist's reactions to a client are an invaluable guide to the presence of narcissistic phenomena. Often, there is a feeling of a lack of real contact or dialogue with the client, who may superficially agree with the therapist's comments, but, with glazed and unresponsive eyes, return to his or her own preoccupations without showing any discernible impact once the therapist has had their say. As a therapist, one may feel bored or excluded, mad or importuning (as though the therapy is for one's own rather than the client's benefit), or even envious of the client, whose life seems so much more colourful and exciting than one's own.

One of the more seductive manifestations of narcissism is to be found in clients who idealise and overvalue therapy and their therapists. They insist on being treated by the top man or woman, the best that is going: nothing less will do. The therapist becomes a saviour, imbued with special powers that compensate for the patient's feelings of ordinariness and insignificance. One therapist, well known for outstanding writing in the field, decided never to take on clients who approached her after reading her work: she found they invariably had projected huge narcissistic longings into her that were often resistant to analysis, and which she was destined to disappoint, not being able to live up to the ideal of the 'perfect therapist' that they thrust upon her.

There are certain characteristic features of more severe narcissism to which we can now turn. In a paper first published in 1922, Abraham focused on 'negative narcissism', in which, paradoxically, sufferers are not so much irredeemably pleased with themselves but, rather, are in a constant state of anxious self-dissatisfaction.[7] What is 'narcissistic' about negative narcissists is that they are just as self-preoccupied as their grandiose cousins, but are locked into self-hatred rather than self-love.

Abraham quotes from Leo Tolstoy's *Boyhood and Youth*:

my occupations . . . included . . . much looking at myself in the glass, from which, however, I always turned away with heavy feelings of depression and even disgust. My outward appearance, I was convinced, was unsightly, and I could not even comfort myself with the usual consolation in such cases – I could not say that my face was expressive, intelligent, or distinguished.[8]

Freud saw the 'negative therapeutic reaction', in which patients deteriorate rather than get better when offered an apposite interpretation of their distressed state, as a manifestation of negative narcissism. For these patients, the 'ideal self' is so far removed from the 'real self' that striving towards it may seem futile – the ideal is too far away to even contemplate. As nothing less than perfection will satisfy, any attempt to change – to lessen the gulf between where one is and where one would like to be – is resisted in order to preserve the relative comfort of the status quo. People are often frightened to change, tending to cling to what they already have, however unsatisfactory it is: there can be a perverse satisfaction in being miserable, if it is familiar.

The origins of such negative narcissism are often to be found in a harsh superego, internalised from parental strictures. One patient described how she came home from school one day, delighted with having achieved 99 per cent in a maths exam, only to be roundly criticised by her father for not getting 100 per cent!

With his libidinal perspective, Freud saw narcissism as a staging post on the way from autoeroticism to object relationships. The unconscious sexual and masturbatory *phantasies* of narcissistic patients (as opposed to their conscious *fantasies*) are important clues to their pathology. In men, there may be a huge preoccupation with the penis, either their own or that of others. Sometimes the narcissist has abandoned hope of mutuality in relationships and relies instead on power and coercion to gain access to his objects, access that provides a sense of security and satisfaction. Sado-masochistic phantasies are common. In female narcissism, the whole body itself may become idealised, with terror and desperation whenever signs of imperfection appear. Fantasies of being made love to by rich and famous men in exotic locations are perhaps a harmless manifestation of normal female narcissism, but some women are in thrall to powerful men, and remain so, however much they suffer as a result. Those who feel powerless and empty, and view themselves as objects to be used, have to meet their narcissistic needs as best they can.

Grandiose phantasies are a normal aspect of adolescent narcissism, but may persist into adulthood, albeit in a highly concealed form. It is rare that a client will speak of such things until they feel they can fully trust the therapist, and, even then, may only do so with much embarrassment and hesitation. Such thoughts are deeply coloured with *shame*, which many, like Phil Mollon, view as the crucial 'narcissistic affect'.[9] The patient may dream of being a famous pop singer, football player, artist, academic, or politician, and of untold riches and power. The possibility of artistic success is particularly seductive to the narcissist because of the social construction of genius. The idea of 'genius' encapsulates the quintessence of narcissism

– someone who is touched by the gods and who can effortlessly achieve great things.

'Narcissistic rage' is another important clinical phenomenon. The narcissist may have managed to construct a world that more or less meets their needs, and in which, to use Freud's famous phrase, 'his majesty the baby'[10] is waited on hand and foot by various courtiers, or at least has found ways to recreate momentary feelings of narcissistic bliss with the aid of drugs, alcohol or sex, or through the purchase of luxury goods. But sooner or later reality will intrude. The sufferer discovers that their needs have to be balanced with those of others, that helpers are motivated not just by devotion but by the necessity of earning a living, or simply that reality has its own logic and does not always bend to the dictates of human will. A therapist may be on holiday just when the patient needs them, or bring a session to an end when the patient is in full flow.

Such phenomena, great or small, may trigger an outburst of narcissistic rage. The patient will metaphorically, or sometimes literally, stamp his foot, smash or trash precious things, or shout the place down. One such patient, whenever he was thwarted, regularly had appalling rows with workmen or fellow drivers who got in his way on narrow lanes. In therapy he appeared compliant and accepting, but it gradually emerged how much he deeply resented and took personally the therapist's holiday breaks, which he felt were invariably calculated to come at a time when he was most in need of support and comfort. As a child he had hour-long outbursts in which he threw himself inconsolably to the ground and screamed himself sick. With unempathic parents and having spent long periods in hospital during his childhood, he was enormously insecure, and, like Fisher-Mamblona's gosling Feli,[11] appeared to be catapulted into fits of rage whenever he felt threatened, as a form of 'displacement activity'. (This term refers to an apparently irrelevant set of behaviours triggered by intense emotions that cannot be 'directly' discharged or dealt with at the time.) The rage itself seems to provide a measure of security for the narcissist who is fundamentally so lonely and deprived of a secure base.

Beneath narcissistic rage lies what Mollon terms 'narcissistic vulnerability' or, as Kohut calls it, the 'narcissistic wound'. The narcissist is caught in a bind whose limits are the universal need to feel special on the one hand, and the equally imperative need to adapt to reality on the other. An attempt is made to create a world which will boost their sense of specialness and importance, but underneath lurks despair and depression and feelings of insignificance. In these circumstances, the narcissist is vulnerable to even minor slights and rejections which disconfirm their specialness, as well as to the everyday, or sometimes extraordinary, mishaps and traumas which unrelenting fate decrees.

Two contrasting clinical patterns of narcissism have been described. Rosenfeld's 'thick-' and 'thin-skinned' narcissists become, in Glenn Gabbard's terminology, the 'oblivious' and the 'hypervigilant'.[12] *Oblivious* narcissists appear to have little understanding of others' feelings and ride roughshod with their arrogant and self-serving ruthlessness. They are grandiose and exhibition-istic in their manner. *Hypervigilant* types are shy, inhibited and self-centred in their sensitivity to rejection or criticism. They seem to have 'one skin missing', and are so easily emotionally bruised that their self intrudes in every encounter. Anthony Bateman argues that these stereotypes are not mutually exclusive and that the hypervigilant are far less fragile than they appear, with huge rage lying not far beneath their frailty, while seemingly oblivious people, once engaged in therapy, may ultimately reveal emptiness and despair.[13]

Literary Examples of Narcissism

Ovid's version of the Narcissus myth

Many contemporary ideas about narcissism can be found in embryonic form in the classical Narcissus myth which gave its name to the syndrome. Here, I follow Ted Hughes' powerful translation of the Ovid version.[14]

The story starts not with Narcissus but with

Tiresias, the only person to have lived both as male and female, and whom Jove and Juno therefore called in to adjudicate in their dispute over who derived the greater pleasure from the act of sex: man or woman. Tiresias' vote was for women. (Although in some versions he diplomatically replies that while women experience ten times the intensity of pleasure, men experience it ten times more often!) Juno, inexplicably angry, strikes him blind, while to compensate, Jove opens Tiresias' *inner* eye, giving him the gift of prophecy. Thus Ovid reveals the narcissistic themes of bodily pleasure, envy, and the difficulty in knowing how another truly feels, especially when one is oneself consumed with desire.

Narcissus was the product of his mother Liriope's rape by the river-god Cephisus. Narcissus was outstandingly beautiful from birth, so much so that envious gossips came to Tiresias questioning whether a creature so beautiful could live for long. Here the profound theme of the transience of beauty, and of the links between narcissism, envy and death is introduced.

Tiresias answers enigmatically: he can live long, *'unless he learns to know himself'*. The paradox turns on the fatal word 'unless'. The terrible dilemma of the narcissist is thus elegantly summarised: either the narcissist remains trapped forever in the shadow world of self-love, or he is released from the bondage of self-unknowing (and by implication being unable to know others), but on price of death. Although the narcissist thinks only of himself, ironically he can never really know himself, since he cannot take a position outside himself and see himself as he 'really' is. If he could accept that beauty fades then his loveliness would be something to celebrate; by grandiosely denying the reality of loss and change, this beauty is transformed into monstrosity.

Narcissus grows into a beautiful young man. Many fall in love with him, but he keeps his distance. Then the wood-nymph Echo sees him and is immediately stricken. Previously a chatterbox, she has lost her power of speech as punishment from her mother Juno who discovered that Echo was being used as a decoy by Jove to engage her in conversation while he was away chasing other women. All she can do is repeat the words she has just heard. How is she to declare her love? One day Narcissus is lost in woods and calls out to his friends: 'Come to me.' Echo reveals herself: 'to me', 'to me', she calls. Narcissus turns and runs: 'I would rather be dead than let you touch me.' Echo is mortified, and slowly dies of lost love, until all that is left is her voice.

Narcissists break hearts. They cannot see the impact of their actions on others. They attract flatterers and fawners, themselves narcissistically traumatised, hoping for reflected glory. Echo's 'God-mother' (Juno) is so envious of her relationship with her 'God-father' (Jove) that she blights the father–daughter relationship so essential to healthy female narcissism – a relationship in which the adolescent daughter knows that her father sees her as beautiful, but where, at the same time, he is utterly respectful of her sexuality.

Echo, the hypervigilant, becomes the mirror image of the oblivious Narcissus. He is untouchable; she eternally longs to be in his arms. He thinks only of himself and is ruthlessly selfish; she can only think of him, and her damaged self-esteem remains fragile even unto her death. He cannot identify with others and so make their voices his own, thereby enlarging the range of his personality; she has no voice of her own, and is condemned to pale imitation. In attachment terms, both are anxiously attached: she clings insufferably to her object, he forever keeps his at a distance.

Many others fall unrequitedly in love with Narcissus. Eventually one, in a crucial therapeutic move, has the courage to confront his tormentor. (It is a 'his' – there is a suggestion of bisexuality throughout the myth, as though Narcissus cannot be content with the love of only one sex.)

Let Narcissus love and suffer
As he has made us suffer
Let him, like us, love and know it is hopeless . . .[15]

One day, thirsty from hunting, Narcissus finds a 'pool of perfect water' and there, as he stretches out to drink:

A strange new thirst, a craving, unfamiliar,
Entered his body with the water,
And entered his eyes
With the reflection in the limpid mirror . . .
As the taste of water flooded him
So did love.[16]

He falls deeply in love with his own image. But the harder he tries to embrace himself, to kiss the lips that 'seemed to be rising to kiss his', the more frustrated and lovesick he becomes. He bemoans his fate. Eternally separated from his love-object, he experiences loss and grief for the first time. At last he comes to know himself:

You are me. Now I see that . . .
But it is too late.
I am in love with myself . . .
This is a new kind of lover's prayer
To wish himself apart from the one he loves.[17]

He realises that he must die: 'I am a cut flower', 'Let death come quickly'. At last he feels compassion for another: 'The one I loved should be let live. He should live on after me, blameless.' But he knows this is impossible. When he dies, both he and his observing self die – and even as he crosses the Styx he cannot resist a glimpse of himself in the water. But at the moment of his death he is transformed – metamorphosed – into a beautiful flower. To this day, the narcissus, with its evanescent delicate trumpet and seductive fragrance, is a tribute to Tiresias' prescience.

Tiresias, like a good psychotherapist, knew that if we are to survive psychologically, we must outgrow our narcissism. If we can accept our own transience and mortality, then we can be transformed – our self-esteem will be secure and we will be blessed with an inner beauty. If not, we are condemned to a living or actual death, perhaps at our own hands, as our narcissism grows ever more demanding and insistent. We will grow a thick skin over the vulnerability which has made us shy away from relationships. Loving only ourselves we envy those who can relate to others, and do our damnedest to destroy them, using our beauty as a weapon.

Shakespeare: Sonnet 62

For Shakespeare's protagonist, the act of writing is
a process of self-discovery:

Sin of self-love possesseth all mine eye,
And all my soul, and all my every part;
And for this sin there is no remedy,
It is so grounded inward in my heart.

(62: 1–4)

There is perhaps an ironic tone here. Is it really
such a sin to love oneself? Well-founded healthy
narcissism needs to be 'grounded in the heart' if it
is to serve its purpose, and to keep us buoyant in
the face of life's tribulations. And yet the narcissist
who has eyes only for himself is lost. He is
consumed with envy, constantly having to boost
himself by comparing himself with others. Like
Snow White's step-mother, he boasts:

Methinks no face so gracious is as mine . . .
As I all other in all worths surmount.

(62: 5, 8)

What is more – and here's the rub – when age creeps in, all is lost, as self-love turns to self-loathing:

But when my glass shows me myself indeed,
Beated and chapped with tanned antiquity,
Mine own self-love quite contrary I read;
Self so self-loving were iniquity.

(62: 9–12)

The resolution comes in the final couplet which, like Tiresias' paradox, depends on a metamorphosis:

'Tis thee, my self, that for myself I praise,
Painting my age with the beauty of thy days.

(62: 13–14)

The solution to narcissism is to love another. But, unlike Narcissus who longs for some separation between lover and beloved, Shakespeare highlights the merging aspect of love. 'Thee' and 'my self' form a unity in which there is no distinction between self and other, in which self-love and object-love come together, or as Freud put it:

a real happy love corresponds to the primal condition [i.e. of early infancy] *in which object-libido and ego-libido cannot be distinguished . . .*[18]

Being in love both destroys and preserves narcissism, in the practical sense that to love is to escape from oneself, but also helps one to feel good about oneself; and in the theoretical sense that self-love passes over, and so is lost, via projective identification, into the image of the beloved, where it is metamorphosed into a celebration of their existence. The 'paint' of the ageing, perhaps theatrical, narcissist – the makeup, rejuvenating creams and cosmetic surgery – is transformed by mutual happiness and the hue of the loved one.

This sonnet was probably written to Shakespeare's young and handsome noble patron. Thus while offering a partial solution to the inherent problem of narcissism – transience – it could be seen as narcissistic in that it is based on the love of a younger man by an older one, who projects all his own narcissism into youth.

In Freud's schema:

A person may love according to the narcissistic type:
- *(a)   what he himself is (i.e. himself)*
- *(b)   what he himself was*
- *(c)   what he himself would like to be . . .*[19]

Narcissus, and the poet at the start of the Sonnet are in category (a). The penultimate line of the poem suggests that all types of love – certainly all falling in love – contain an element of narcissism in that the beauty is as much in the eye of the beholder as in the separateness of the beloved. The last line suggests that movement from (a) to (b) or (c) may represent progress but still remains within the bounds of narcissism. Taken with Ovid, we can suggest that truly relational love depends on the capacity for both merging and separation. Unlike narcissistic and 'echoistic' love, such love is both eternal and transient, depending on the capacity simultaneously to trust and to cope with separation and loss.

Wilde: The Picture of Dorian Gray

All three of Freud's varieties of narcissism are amply illustrated in Wilde's novel *The Picture of Dorian Gray* (1891), which was doubtless stimulated by contemporary fascination with 'alters' and doppelgangers. It contains one of the classic images of narcissism – the diabolic pact in which the narcissist defeats ageing by presenting an eternally youthful face to the world, while the true horror of his inner self is depicted in a grotesque portrait, locked away in his innermost attic sanctum.

The novel starts with a series of epigrammatic statements about Art. These are essentially anti-puritanical celebrations of the 'uselessness' of art and the supreme importance of beauty as a virtue in its own right. They represent another of the metamorphoses of narcissism. By transforming his narcissism into Art, Wilde transcends its self-centredness, since 'artistic beauty' (as opposed to 'real beauty') does not fade and is a form of communication. Even destructive narcissism finds justification: 'Vice and virtue are to the artist materials for an art.'[20]

The novel centres on three main characters, each of whom perhaps represents a facet of Wilde's personality. Dorian – the golden boy – is an incredibly beautiful young man; Lord Henry Wootton, a forerunner of Algernon in *The Importance of Being Earnest*, is a witty and ruthless *roué* who takes Dorian under his wing; Basil Hallward is the painter touched with dangerous genius, whose portrait of Dorian has such magical properties.

Dorian gazes at his portrait, and imagines a Faustian pact:

How sad it is! I shall grow old, and horrible and dreadful. But this picture will always remain young. It will never be older than this particular day of June . . . If it were only the other way! For that I would give everything . . . I would give my soul for that![21]

The novel turns on the interplay of Wootton and Dorian's narcissism. Each is enormously excited by the other: Gray by Wootton's intellect and social ease, Wootton by Gray's looks and innocence, and by the fact that he is able to manipulate him at will. Dorian falls in love with a pretty young actress, Sibyl Vane, but like a true narcissist he has no real feelings for her, and is merely excited by the idea of possessing someone who is so admired by everyone else. In this way she vicariously enlarges the scope of his narcissism, and her love for him is flattering. But then, to his horror, he realises that others find her ordinary and lacking in talent. The mundane and socially inferior concerns of a real person begin to intrude and he drops her. Mortified, she commits suicide, which tips Gray into a life of debauchery and viciousness. Rosenfeld's mafia gang has taken over his personality, and there is no escape. While his looks remain unchanged, the secret portrait reveals the cruelty and ugliness of his soul.

As the novel descends into Gothic horror, Hallward visits Dorian in a vain attempt to get him to mend his ways. Gray reveals the 'omnipotence' and grandiosity of the narcissist: 'I shall show you my soul. You shall see the things you fancy only God can see.'[22] Then Gray confronts Hallward with the despair of the narcissist. Like Narcissus when he finally realises that his ever elusive beloved is none other than himself, now Gray grasps how his pursuit of eternal youth has condemned him to cause and to suffer unutterable misery. Hallward offers him the chance to repent, but destructiveness takes over and Gray stabs the artist to death. Gray manages to escape the revenge of Sybil's brother, and shows some slight stirrings of redemption as he decides not to exploit another lovesick woman, Hetty Merton. He revisits the picture in the hope that this act of charity will show in a softening of his image, but it is too late: his sins cannot be wiped out so easily. His final act is to plunge the murder knife into the magical canvas. As he does this, he falls, stricken, so that in the morning his servants find an old and ugly man dead on the floor, with the portrait mysteriously intact, now depicting the bloom of youth from the moment it was painted twenty years before.

The narcissist is likely to become suicidal at the moment of narcissistic collapse. *Dorian Gray* is grotesque because in it the normal relationship between phantasy and reality is reversed. The seductiveness of Art lies in its capacity to create an artificial reality that is both an expression of narcissism and, through self-knowledge, a release from it. Thus in Seamus Heaney's poem 'Personal Helicon', he describes his fascination with wells as a child, into which, 'big-eyed Narcissus', he would stare endlessly. He compares this with his adult activity as a poet in which: 'I rhyme/To see myself, to set the darkness echoing.'[23]

Theorising Narcissism

Theories about narcissism have stimulated fierce debate within psychoanalysis and centre on two main issues. The first concerns the relationship between primary and secondary narcissism, the second about the healthiness, or otherwise, of narcissistic phenomena in general.

Primary and secondary narcissism

Freud differentiated *primary narcissism*, a normal developmental stage in early infancy en route to states of object relatedness, from *secondary narcissism* in which troubled individuals regressively take themselves as their primary love-object rather than another. Secondary narcissism is relatively uncontentious. It covers the range of different conditions described earlier in which people are pathologically self-preoccupied; unable to relate; approach others not as ends in themselves but as means to selfish ends; resort to 'self-soothing' behaviours such as drug addiction, deliberate self-harm or promiscuous sex; become self-defeatingly self-reliant, and so on.

The main debate has focused on the precise meaning of the term primary narcissism, and whether it refers to any real phenomenon. Freud's original idea was that the child – after the stage of autoeroticism, but before becoming aware of his mother as a separate being, and therefore as someone to love (or 'libidinally cathect') in her own right – narcissistically invests himself with the love he had felt from his mother. Later, however, Freud used the term in a more general sense to denote an undifferentiated state of existence, occurring before the child has developed even a rudimentary ego or self.[24] In this state, the infant basks in maternal tenderness and care, and is suffused with blissful feelings of love and being loved that are neither object- or self-directed, or are perhaps both at the same time.

As psychoanalysis has moved from a libido-oriented to an interpersonal perspective this concept has been challenged. Michael Balint and Ronald Fairbairn argue that we are object related from the start of life,[25] and research by Stern on infant behaviour seems to support this view.[26] Infants interact intensively with their mothers from birth and can for example differentiate the smell of their own mother's milk from that of others in the first few hours of life. Melanie Klein argues that young babies have an ego that is actively involved in mental processes such as splitting, idealisation and denigration. In this schema there seems little room for the notion of primary narcissism. As Symmington roundly puts it, 'the only narcissism that exists . . . is secondary narcissism'.[27]

Even the original conceptualisation of secondary narcissism is questionable. Freud saw homosexuality, psychosis, and hypochondria as examples of secondary narcissism in which libido is directed inwardly to the self, rather than outwards to another. Today, few would argue that people suffering from schizophrenia do not form object relationships. They are, if anything, interpersonally over-sensitive. Similarly crude distinctions between homosexual and heterosexual types of loving are utterly outdated. Many homosexuals form mature loving relationships, and, conversely, heterosexual object choice is not infrequently narcissistic, in the sense of choosing a glamorous 'trophy partner' whose main psychological role is to boost the subject's narcissism through stimulating envy in others.

Healthy versus pathological narcissism

In the late 1960s Kohut mounted an important challenge to the (then conventional) views on narcissism. Kohut argued that Freud's idea – of a single developmental line from narcissism to object relationship – should be abandoned. For him, the growth and shaping of normal healthy narcissism is a separate and necessary developmental process in its own right. Rather than seeing narcissism as a 'bad' thing, to be found in the mentally ill, immature and those not properly analysed, he argued that healthy narcissism is a precondition of successful living, including object relating, and that the phenomena of secondary narcissism should be considered as representing 'breakdown products' of the normal process of narcissistic maturation.

Kohut quotes Freud's famous statement that: 'a man who has been the undisputed favourite of his mother keeps for life the feeling of a conqueror; that confidence of success often induces real success', and from a chapter entitled 'Baby Worship' in Anthony Trollope's *Barchester Towers* in which a mother is looking at her little boy:

'Diddle, diddle . . . dum . . . hasn't he got lovely legs?' . . . Said the rapturous mother '. . . He's a little . . . darling, so he is; and he has the nicest little pink legs in all the world . . .'[28]

My own research shows how often this process appears to have gone wrong in the infancy of people destined later to suffer from narcissistic and Borderline personality disorders. Such sufferers believe either that they were unwanted, or an 'afterthought', or were adopted; that their mothers had 'terrible' labours which made them determined never to have another child; that they were responsible for their mothers' post-natal depression, or for causing their fathers to walk out. All this suggests a narcissistic self that has been blighted from birth.

When things go right, the child begins to build up a sense of himself as special and lovable, and is able to enjoy healthy exhibitionism, and grandiosity. A child aged three who jumps off a sofa onto a soft landing, shouting to his parents 'Look at me, I can fly!', will be admired with affectionate pride. When that child goes to school a year or two later, his parents will collect him from the school gate with a 'gleam' in their eye – seeing their own child standing out from the crowd as though suffused with a special light. If parents cannot love their children in this way, then the seeds of shame and self-disgust are sown.

Kohut coined the word 'selfobject' to describe this specialness of intimate relationships in which the other is neither fully part of the self, nor fully separate. A young child's parents are selfobjects, in that they are experienced as extensions of the self which the child can to some degree control. This selfobject relationship can be seen as purely illusory and defensive – a way of avoiding the traumatic realisation of the helplessness and vulnerability of childhood. For Kohut, however, selfobjecthood is an antidote to the excessive preoccupation with autonomy and separateness which he sees as pathologically endemic in Western culture.

As development proceeds, so infantile grandiosity (or 'omnipotence') and exhibitionism have to be tempered with reality and self-awareness. Kohut calls this 'optimal frustration', and states:

If the child is spoiled (not optimally frustrated), it retains an unusual amount of narcissism or omnipotence; and at the same time because it lacks actual skills, feels inferior. Similarly, overly frustrating experiences . . . lead to retention of omnipotence fantasies.[29]

Getting the right balance between necessary frustration and a shameful awareness of helplessness is a skilful task, and one which, according to Kohut, is best done by more than one parent: from a classical oedipal perspective it is the father's role to frustrate the child's sense of exclusive possession of the mother. At the same time the father, or 'paternal principle' (which can equally be provided by the mother herself or a male relation), helps the child to metamorphose his grandiosity and exhibitionism into what Kohut calls the 'bipolar self', whose twin poles are the ideals to which we strive, and ambition – a word Kohut uses for the sense of real potency (as opposed to delusions of omnipotent control) in achieving those ideals. Again, it is noteworthy how frequently the childhood of Borderline patients is characterised by abusive, drunken or disappearing fathers – and often all three.

The ultimate blow to narcissism is the fact of our own death; coming to terms with death is a mark of maturity and wisdom. For Kohut, narcissism, successfully negotiated, leads to the capacity to accept mortality, to see oneself as one is without over- or underestimation, to develop a sense of creativity and humour and to trust one's intuition and empathy. The paradox of this process is that narcissism needs to be healthily established before it can be given up.

Donald Winnicott wrote famously about a child's use of a spoon during a consultation: holding it, sucking it, hitting with it.[30] Victoria Hamilton similarly emphasises the infant's acquisition of the ability to *grasp* an object as illustrating both healthy narcissism and its transcendence.[31] Grasping is a huge achievement for a small child and often seems to produce a sense of mastery and satisfaction – there is a triumphant look in the child's eye as he manages to wrest his cup from the high-chair table and bring it to his mouth for the first time. At the same time, grasping is an escape from the solipsism of infancy – an encounter with the real world that carries through into the metaphorical use of the word: to denote our ability to comprehend ideas. 'Spoiling' a child – helping too much, in a way that compromises autonomy – interferes with this process of discovery of the world.

In the Kohutian schema, defective narcissism is as problematic as excessive narcissism, and pathology arises when normal selfobject development is inhibited. A modicum of what Britton calls 'epistemic narcissism' – an unshakable belief in the rightness of one's own ideas – is the mark of a creative and assertive self. For Britton however, as a follower of Rosenfeld, such epistemic narcissism is essentially defensive. In 'destructive narcissism' the sufferer feels so threatened by the existence of people outside himself upon whom he depends, and feels so envious of them, that in order to maintain his omnipotent position as 'lord of all he surveys' he must eradicate the object forthwith. The pathological aspects of narcissism – treating others as a means to an end, ruthless self-centredness, lack of empathy – are all manifestations of this envious need to deny the importance of the object.

The mirror image of this thick-skinned narcissism is to be found in the utterly vulnerable patient who controls her object by remorselessly tugging at their heart strings. Leslie Sohn's metaphor of the Pied Piper who lures all the healthy children into the mountainside, leaving only the crippled boy behind, captures the way in which such patients may present only the wounded part of themselves to the therapist, while the healthy aspects are inaccessibly sequestered, emerging perhaps unwittingly in dreams and scraps of creativity.[32]

Kernberg similarly emphasises the pathological aspects of narcissism, in which he postulates a 'grandiose self comprising a fusion of real self, ideal self and ideal object, and resulting in an idealised self-sufficiency, making the subject impervious to intimate relationships, including analysis'. According to Kernberg, the narcissist is saying:

I do not need to fear that I will be rejected for not living up to the ideal of myself which alone makes it possible for me to be loved by the ideal person I imagine would love me. That ideal person and my ideal image of that person and my real self are all one and better than the ideal person whom I wanted to love me, so that I do not need anybody else any more.[33]

Or, as the nursery rhyme has it: 'I care for nobody, no not I, for nobody cares for me.'

The radical self-sufficiency of the narcissist is of course in direct denial of the inescapable fact of parental sex – the ultimate act to which we owe our existence and over which we have no control ('I did not ask to be born' is the despairing cry of depressed narcissism). The narcissist strives to think of himself as a 'self-made man', but may pay the price of inability to allow the 'free intercourse of unconscious parts of the mind – free association'.[34]

In sum, the narcissistic self comprises three layers of feelings: an outer denial of dependency and a consequent self-admiration; beneath which lies overwhelming oral rage and envy; and below that, a frustrated yearning for loving care.

Attachment approaches to narcissism

'Attachment theory' brings an empirical approach to bear on psychoanalysis.[35] It emphasises the importance of protection and security provided by the care-giver (usually the mother), for the child, who turns to a 'secure base' when threatened. Can attachment theory, with its emphasis on evidence and observation, help reconcile the Kernbergian and Kohutian perspectives? Attachment theory makes a clear distinction between healthy and sub-optimal developmental lines, which it sees as being established quite early in the course of psychological growth, so that by one year, children can be divided into those with secure and those with insecure attachment patterns. Insecure attachment is seen as a defensive response to sub-optimal parenting – a way of maintaining contact with a supposedly 'secure' base that is in fact rejecting, inconsistent or psychologically confused and unavailable. This produces the characteristic patterns of insecurity: avoidant, ambivalent (clinging), and disorganised.[36]

In secure attachment the mother is responsive and attuned. As Winnicott put it, her face is the mirror in which the infant begins to find and know itself.[37] Healthy narcissism starts from the warm responsive mirror-mother who is able accurately to reflect back the infant's feelings which form the core of the self. Through the presence of another we can come to know and accept ourselves. Where attachment is insecure, this mirroring process is compromised. The mirror may be blank and unresponsive (leading to the avoidant pattern);

suffused with the parent's feelings rather than those of the infant (ambivalent pattern); or chaotic and confusing (disorganised pattern).

Narcissus and Echo could be seen as typifying the avoidant and ambivalent strategies. As her son was the product of a rape, Liriope may have had difficult feelings about Narcissus from the start. This 'ghost in the nursery'[38] meant that her helpless rage towards his father may have led to an aggressive care-giving pattern, in which Narcissus, seeking some sort of security, will have suppressed his loving feelings and tried to become emotionally self-sufficient. He may have denied the reality of parental sex that led to his existence, and in phantasy seen himself as self-generated. His beauty ensured that this relationship with himself would always be on offer, but his own suppressed rage about rejection by his mother meant that he could not trust an other and thereby establish a secure base, preferring to use people in a punishing and coercive way instead. At school or with his peers, Narcissus would have been a bully, picking on victims like Echo as his prey.

Echo, by contrast, illustrates ambivalent attachment: her self exists only in response to others, never as an active agent. Her narcissism is in this metamorphic sense anti-narcissistic. Her only hope is to cling to the object in order to achieve a modicum of security.

As development proceeds, so external attachment patterns with care-givers are internalised as representations of Self, Other, and their varying relationship (for example, the distressed self, and secure or insecure responses from the 'secure base'). These representations in turn colour relationships with significant others. This whole process depends in part on the care-giver's capacity to see the child as a separate sentient being. For all their difficulties, at least Narcissus and Echo have coherent selves, albeit based around insistent self-sufficiency or compulsive caring, respectively. For the avoidant Narcissus, this will feed into a grandiose self; for the ambivalent Echo, a depleted self. Insofar as Narcissus denies the importance of the secure base and takes himself as his object, he will demonstrate clinical features of narcissism. Echo will be vulnerable to dependency and negative narcissism; her only security, in the sense of an internal object to which she can cling, is a denigratory superego – derived from Juno's rage.

Avoidant and ambivalent strategies involve either the absorption of some of the functions of the necessary Other into the self, or the 'projection' of self-characteristics onto the clung-to object, attributing to the other one's own qualities. By contrast, without a consistent means to achieve even partial security, the 'disorganised' individual resorts to bizarre methods to approximate to a secure base. Disorganised people lack a coherent representation of the Other, and have to rely on various forms of self-splitting to create a secure base effect. In 'narcissistic' phenomena such as cutting the body with razor blades (for example, in Borderline Personality Disorder), or self-starvation (in anorexia nervosa), the body becomes an 'Other' to which the sufferer relates, albeit in a pathological way.

Psychological and to some extent physical

survival depends on the ability to form a close attachment relationship and thereby to achieve an external secure base in reality, and an 'internal secure base' within the self.[39] The relationship with this secure base is healthily narcissistic, in the sense that the other is seen to be there for the benefit and security of the subject. The establishment of this base is a precondition for seeing the other as a separate being, and for having fun together and exploring the world in a companionable way – in short, for establishing an object relationship.

The clinical phenomena of narcissism can be seen as attempts to use the self as a secure base surrogate. For the hypervigilant, 'Echoic', person this means taking the body and/or the Self as the secure base, clinging to it in an escalating cycle, since the more it is clung to, the more questionable it seems as a source of security, and so the more insistent the clinging. The oblivious narcissist has taken a different route to partial security. Despairing of mutuality, he relies on coercion and power to maintain some sort of relationship with others. His own fundamental powerlessness creates unbearable envy, so, turning the tables, he evokes envy in others, and thus excites their attention, albeit from a distance.

An integrative perspective:
The emergence and metamorphoses
of narcissism

Eric Erikson's model of the growth of the mind visualises a series of stages, each with its own positive or negative polarity: basic trust versus mistrust; autonomy versus shame and doubt; industry versus inferiority; generativity versus stagnation; integrity versus despair.[40] In concluding this section, I offer a similar model to integrate the various aspects of narcissism, both healthy and pathological. The stages described are necessarily artificial, and not superseded, merely added to, as development proceeds. Each can be activated at any time.

Stage 1, first year of life – secure sense of creative self in relation to a responsive other.

The crucial issue here is parental attunement: empathy, mirroring, and responsiveness. Treated with ordinary parental devotion, the child feels himself as 'special', unique, the centre of his own universe. He is a distinct sentient being, in relation to responsive others. Knowing that his word is his care-giver's command, he can begin to tolerate periods of frustration and separation. He is helped to reach out to the world and to trust that he will be met with acceptance and joy. Here the beginnings of good self-esteem, or healthy narcissism, are installed. Conversely, in the absence of parental attunement the child may experience feelings of inner emptiness, dread, insignificance, impotence and periods of inconsolable rage. A temperamentally difficult or physically imperfect child may be at particular risk here.

Stage 2, second year of life – narcissistic investment in the body and its growing powers.
Healthy exhibitionism arises at this stage. Parents delight as their children reach developmental milestones, as they begin to walk, talk, gain

sphincter control, and to explore the world. The secure base is not just a source of security but of encouragement and approbation. The child invests his body with the glow of healthy narcissism, and enjoys the gleam in the parental eye as he enters the society of kin and friends. The stressed, depressed, aggressive, rejecting, overwhelmed or resentful parent will denigrate or fail to notice her child's fumbling need to elicit gleam, leading to the beginnings of shame and self-disappointment that is so characteristic of the narcissistically wounded.

Stage 3, third year of life – beginnings of optimal frustration.

Healthy narcissism knows its limitations. A child who is narcissistically entangled with his mother cannot test his hopes and ambitions against reality. The American ideal (and illusion) of 'log cabin to White House' has to be tempered with the ability to distinguish castles in the air from real dwellings. In the Lacanian schema, the 'Nom (and 'Non') du Pere' – the name and 'no' of the father – both set limits to narcissism, but also help the child to feel that he is part of his parent's clan, and indeed the human race. Individual narcissism begins to be subsumed into social narcissism. Without this process, grandiosity and denial of reality threaten to persist.

Stage 4, adolescence – ideals and ambitions.
Healthy adolescents have their heroes, hopes, ambitions, fervent beliefs and secret dreams. The narcissistically wounded adolescent is in despair and depression, seeing the world as doomed, oppressed by death, and either defying it with risky behaviour or shrinking from it into regressive avoidance. The body becomes a source of pleasure and pride, or else a hated encumbrance that fails to measure up to impossible ideals. An outpouring of creative energy is a mark of healthy self-belief, at this stage not needing to be evaluated or measured up. Rage and destructiveness express narcissistic feelings of failure to find a mirroring ideal.

Stage 5, adulthood – transfer of narcissism to the next generation.

Omnipotence lessens as real potency takes over. The healthy adult begins to know his or her strengths and limitations. He feels good about himself, his relationships, family and society. His narcissistic hopes are invested in his children. Projects are conceived and brought to fruition. Frustrated ideals are replaced with love of truth. Failure is met with acceptance. Meanwhile, the unhealthy narcissist consolidates his self-centred world, either exciting envy or enviously undermining the possibility of intimacy with others. Sufficient unto himself, he becomes more and more self-absorbed – either hyper-vulnerable to every slight, or brutally bullying his way to a 'top' whose twin peaks are his own self-aggrandisement and the denigration of others.

Stage 6, later life – the getting of wisdom.
For Kohut, the installation of healthy narcissism together with optimal frustration sets an individual on a road that leads to the ability to see their world as it is, to accept the reality of one's own death, to trust one's intuition and empathy, find

sources of creativity and humour, and ultimately to achieve a measure of wisdom. In the absence of these metamorphoses, the onset of middle age and beyond raises feelings of terror at one's own inevitable extinction. Depression and hopelessness become ever present possibilities. Narcissism may manifest itself in increasing hypochondria, endless ruminating on past achievements or failures, or a coercive tyranny in which power, rather than mutuality, dominates relationships.

In this health/pathology model, the task of therapy, whatever stage is presented, is to find the seeds of healthy narcissistic strivings, and to reduce the impact of pathological narcissism.

The Psychotherapeutic Treatment of Narcissistic Difficulties

Critics of psychotherapy – perhaps motivated by the puritanism that Wilde so outrageously flouted – accuse it of being self-indulgent, a luxury occupation for those who have nothing better to do with their lives: in other words, of fostering rather than helping to overcome narcissism. Certainly, at its worst, psychotherapy can encourage aspects of psychological life that are typical of narcissism itself: self-preoccupation and interminable regression, an exaggerated sense of entitlement, unrealistic hopes that all past wrongs can be put to rights given sufficient therapeutic love and empathy. This tendency within psychotherapy to become the 'disease of which it purports to be the cure' is yet another of narcissism's metamorphoses, the mirror image of Wilde's self-conscious use of narcissism as an artistic device to overcome narcissism. A more positive view, one which Carl Jung was fond of advocating when contrasting Western with Eastern paths to enlightenment, is that it is necessary to find one's Self before contemplating the possibility of transcending it, and, as the popular phrase has it, you must love yourself before you can begin to love others.

Working with narcissistic patients is difficult in many ways. Here are three vignettes illustrating some of the day-to-day dilemmas they raise for therapists.

Vignette 1:

Bill, a 40-year-old barrister, came into hospital following a near fatal suicide attempt. His career had been hugely successful, but the pleasures of success never seemed to last, and his death-wish came out of a deep sense of dissatisfaction in his marriage, and the realisation of just how cut off he felt from his wife. This was a typical mid-life narcissistic crisis. A great sportsman, bon viveur, womaniser and money-maker, his life felt empty and meaningless. He was referred for psychoanalysis, but it was holiday time and no one could see him for several weeks. He was furious – filled with narcissistic rage. What right had the analysts to be away when he needed help *now*, not in a few weeks' time? If that was the way he was to be treated, let his suicide be on his carers' heads. His ward psychiatrist rang round again, spending quite a long time on the phone, but still to no avail. Bill insisted that he be seen. Why could not the psychiatrist see Bill himself? What was the psychiatrist to do? By agreeing to see Bill, would he be merely pandering to his own narcissism and, like all Bill's conquests, dancing to his self-serving tune? But by refusing to comply with his request, would he not be reinforcing Bill's deep-rooted feeling of not being listened to, throwing him back once more into alienated self-sufficiency?

Vignette 2:

Caroline was both hypervigilant and oblivious. Adopted, she had two older sisters who were her parents' obvious favourites. Her mother became bed-ridden when Caroline was 13 and from then on she was expected to wait on her, and to satisfy her father's sexual needs. She had major depressive breakdowns in her 30s and 40s, and eventually entered weekly supportive psychotherapy which kept her out of hospital and brought some stability into her life. Ending treatment seemed difficult, as she idealised both therapist and therapy, and the compromise was to move to monthly sessions. One of Caroline's characteristic patterns was to 'bolt' when she felt anxious or rejected; on one occasion she took a major overdose and locked herself in the boot of her car, and was only saved by a police helicopter search. Naturally these episodes, usually much milder, caused huge worry to her husband and children whenever she disappeared, and they would immediately start to look for her, not stopping until she was either found or reappeared of her own accord. In one session she was describing a recent example of these episodes, emphasising how unsympathetic her husband had been when eventually he found her. After many years of supportive work, the therapist was suddenly filled with boredom and weary irritation. Without much thought he suggested that perhaps her long-suffering husband was furious with her; he asked her to think about how it must feel for him when she disappeared. Caroline blanched, her lip trembled, she looked frightened and angry, as though she was about to walk out. There was five minutes' silence. Eventually, she decided to stay and the session ended without mishap. At the end she had to pay her bill, and asked to borrow the therapist's pen. She commented on what a nice pen it was – without thinking, the therapist found himself offering it to her as an unwitting present.

Here we see how the thin-skinned narcissist's anger is often projected into those around her; how difficult and dangerous confrontation can be, how important it is to maintain therapeutic potency, how often the 'father-principle' is discarded in favour of a regressive 'maternal' collusion, and how guilty it can make the therapist feel when he does confront such patients.

Vignette 3:

Peter, who had spent most of his childhood in children's homes, was a classic and extreme case of oblivious narcissism, who had lived a life of ruthless selfishness until his late 40s. It was not his depression, violence, alcoholism, lawbreaking habits, loneliness, or declining physical attractiveness to women, but a thin-skinned hypochondria which had led his GP, who had exhausted every pill and physical specialist, to refer him for psychiatric help. As he walked down the corridor to the consulting room, he would invariably start each session by asking in a way that was at once challenging, aggressive, deferential and defensive: 'How are you, doctor?' Finding a way to interpret this apparent concern as another aspect of his narcissism – a need to control the therapeutic situation from the start, as a defence against the threat of relationship formation which being in therapy implied – without alienating and putting him down, was a tough technical challenge.

These examples illustrate some of the common themes of therapy with such people: seductive excitation of the therapist's narcissism; rage and demandingness that can easily stimulate rejection, thereby reinforcing the patient's sense of being let down by everyone but himself; and boredom, again leading to a rejecting neglect of the patient's underlying misery.

Kohut and Kernberg advocate very different ways of handling these issues. Kohut describes three characteristic patterns of transference in therapy with narcissistic patients: mirror transference, idealising transference, and 'twinship' transference. His advice to therapists is along the lines of acceptance and against premature interpretation. As W.B. Yeats put it:

I have spread my dreams under your feet;
tread softly because you tread on my dreams. [41]

The patient must feel able to invest the therapist and therapy with their hopes and dreams. 'Persecutory therapists' who interpret these phantasies as defensive too early and too crashingly, will merely reinforce the narcissistic wound which has led to the need for them in the first place.[42] Kernberg, however, sees dangers in collusion, and emphasises the denigration that is the accompanying shadow of idealisation.[43] He stresses the importance of dealing with negative transference and assisting the patient to develop appropriate concern and guilt for the objects that he uses so thoughtlessly. Patients must be helped to deal with their rage and disappointment, and should not be misled into thinking that therapy can in itself undo past wrongs. Being in therapy stirs up the basic conflicts and deficiencies that have already led to a narcissistic superstructure in the personality. This will arouse a measure of resistance at best, and at worst suicidal feelings. As Rosenfeld puts it:

When he is faced with the reality of being dependent on the analyst, standing for his parents, particularly the mother, he would prefer to die, to be non-existent, to deny the fact of his birth, and also to destroy his analytic progress and insight representing the child in himself, which he feels the analyst, representing the parents, has created.[44]

Kernberg acknowledges, however, that for some patients this will prove too much and that in these cases, in order to maintain a therapeutic alliance, a more supportive approach may be necessary. I end this essay by listing some key principles that I have found can help in working with narcissism in its various manifestations.

• The therapist must be able to accept the idealisation of his relationship with the patient while at the same time not being afraid to challenge the patient's denial of his covert denigration of others' feelings and need for omnipotent control.

- In challenging narcissism, the therapist must guard against using his own position of power and narcissistic superiority to bully and re-inforce the patient's low self-esteem.

- A collusive relationship of mutual admiration must also be eschewed.

- Supporting a patient's narcissism can be a legitimate therapeutic strategy, especially in counteracting compulsive negative narcissism and self-denigration. The therapist must find a positive 'spin' to counterbalance attempts by the patient to do himself down.

- Disillusionment in the therapist and therapy is healthy, but should be gradual rather than traumatic. In time-limited therapy, the ending should be discussed and interpreted right from the start.

- The therapist must be able to set limits both to the demandingness of the thin-skinned and the fury of the thick-skinned narcissist.

- Creativity, humour, playfulness and the use of dreams are all positive manifestations of transformed narcissism and are crucial ingredients of therapy.

- Curiosity about the therapist may be part of the omnipotent need to control or to enviously cut him down to size, but is also a potentially healthy escape from self-preoccupation into wishing to know about the world.

- Gratitude comes late in the therapy of narcissism.

- The gap between actual and ideal self is distorted in narcissism. In the ambivalent, 'Echoic', negative, hypervigilant type, the gap is too great. In the 'Narcissistic', thick-skinned, oblivious type, there is fusion of Ego and Ego-Ideal. The therapeutic task is to narrow the gap in the former, helping the sufferer to find and accept good things about himself; in the latter to open it up, helping the patient to come to terms with loss and failure.

- The two types are not mutually exclusive. Beneath the thick skin of the narcissist, there is huge vulnerability and longing for closeness; below the fragility and pitifulness of the hypervigilant type, there is often ruthless self-centredness.

- The narcissist seeks his object in the mirror, but is doomed to disappointment as the mirror is cold and lifeless and cannot rescue him from his loneliness. Therapy can transform narcissism through 'mirroring' – the playful, warm, responsive mirroring of the attuned Other.

In conclusion, Freud, narcissistically perhaps, saw psychoanalysis as the third of the three great blows that civilisation has dealt to man's narcissism: the Copernican revolution, which displaced the earth from the centre of the universe; the Darwinian revolution, which dethroned Man from his superiority over the rest of Nature; and the psychoanalytic, in which the conscious mind is demoted to a servant of the unconscious forces that rule our lives. To this, an attachment perspective might add a fourth blow: the understanding of how, at a very fundamental level, our prized individuality arises out of our relationships with others. In each case, the miracle of transformed narcissism leads to deeper understanding: we see the beauty and simplicity of the universe; realise the extent to which we are linked with, rather than excluded from, nature; understand how we are psychologically all of a piece; and that, rather than divided and isolated selves, we are inescapably interconnected.

Notes

1. Rycroft, C., *Critical Dictionary of Psychoanalysis*, London: Penguin, 1972.

2. See Lasch, C., *The Culture of Narcissism*, New York: Doubleday, 1979.

3. Britton, R., *Belief and Imagination*, London: Routledge, 1998.

4. Rosenfeld, H., *Psychotic States: A Psycho Analytic Approach,* New York: International Universities Press, 1965.

5. Kohut, H., *The Analysis of the Self*, New York: International Universities Press, 1971.

6. Freud, S., 'On Narcissism' (1914), in *Standard Edition of the Complete Psychological Works of Sigmund Freud*, Vol. 14, trans. James Strachey, London: Hogarth Press, 1953–73, p. 91.

7. Abraham, K., *Selected Papers of Karl Abraham*, London: Hogarth Press, 1973.

8. Tolstoy, L., quoted in Abraham, quoted in Hamilton, V., *Narcissus and Oedipus*, London: Routledge, 1982, pp. 122–3.

9. Mollon, P., *The Fragile Self*, London: Whurr, 1993.

10. Freud, S., op. cit., p. 91.

11. Fisher-Mamblona, H., 'On the evolution of attachment-disordered behaviour', in *Attachment and Human Development*, 2, 2000, pp. 8–21.

12. Gabbard, G., *Psychodynamic Psychiatry in Clinical Practice*, Washington: American Psychiatric Press, 1996.

13. Bateman, A., 'Thick- and thin-skinned organisations and enactment in borderline and narcissistic disorders', in *International Journal of Psycho-Analysis*, 79, 1998, pp. 13–26.

14. Hughes, T., *Tales from Ovid*, London: Faber and Faber, 1997.

15. Ovid, in Hughes, T., op. cit.

16. Ibid.

17. Ibid.

18. Freud, S., op. cit., p. 100.

19. Ibid., p. 90.

20. Wilde, O., *The Picture of Dorian Gray* (1891), London: Penguin, 1985.

21. Ibid., p. 31.

22. Ibid., p. 168.

23. Heaney, S., *Opened Ground: Poems 1966–1996*, London: Faber and Faber, 1998, p. 15.

24. Laplanche, J. and Pontalis, J-B., *The Language of Psychoanalysis*, London: Hogarth Press, 1980.

25. Balint, M., *The Basic Fault*, London: Hogarth Press, 1968; Fairbairn, R., *Collected Papers*, London: Hogarth Press, 1952.

26. Stern, D., *The Interpersonal World of the Infant*, New York: Basic Books, 1985.

27. Symmington, N., *Emotion and Spirit,* London: Karnac, 1993, p. 120.

28. Both quotes taken from Kohut, H., in Morrison, A. (ed.), *Essential Papers on Narcissism*, New York: New York University Press, 1986, pp. 69–70.

29. Kohut, H. and Seitz, P., 'Three Self Psychologies – or One?', in Goldberg, A. (ed.), *The Evolution of Self Psychology: Progress in Self Psychology*, Vol. 7, Hillsdale, NY: Analytic Press, 1963, p. 20.

30. Winnicott, D., *Playing and Reality,* London: Penguin, 1971.

31. Hamilton, V., op. cit.

32. Sohn, L., 'Narcissistic organisation, projective identification, and the formation of the "identificate"', in *International Journal of Psycho-Analysis*, 66, 1985, pp. 201–13.

33. Kernberg, O., in Morrison, op. cit., pp. 134–5.

34. Mollon, P., op. cit., p. 109.

35. See Bowlby, J., *A Secure Base*, London: Routledge, 1988.

36. Holmes, J. and Harrison-Hall, A., forthcoming, 2001.

37. Winnicott, D., *The Maturational Processes and the Facilitating Environment*, London: Hogarth Press, 1968.

38. Fraiberg, S., Adelson, E. and Shapiro, V., 'Ghosts in the nursery: a psychoanalytic approach to impaired

infant–mother relationships', *Journal of American Academy of Child Psychologists*, Vol. 14, 1975, pp. 387–422.

39. Holmes, J., *The Search for the Secure Base*, London: Routledge, 2001.

40. Erikson, E., *Identity, Youth and Crisis*, London: Faber and Faber, 1968.

41. Yeats, W.B. , 'He wishes for the cloths of heaven', in *Collected Poems*, London: Macmillan, 1972.

42. Meares, R. and Hobson, R., 'The persecutory therapist', in *British Journal of Medical Psychology*, 50, 1977, pp. 349–59.

43. Kernberg, O., *Borderline Conditions and Pathological Narcissism*, New York: New York Universities Press, 1975.

44. Rosenfeld, H., 'A clinical approach to the psychoanalytic theory of the life and death instincts: an investigation into the aggressive aspects of narcissism', in Spillius, E. (ed.), *Melanie Klein Today*, Vol. 1, London: Routledge, 1988, p. 247.

Further Reading

Abraham, K., *Selected Papers of Karl Abraham*, London: Hogarth Press, 1973.

Balint, M., *The Basic Fault*, London: Hogarth Press, 1968.

Britton, R., *Belief and Imagination*, London: Routledge, 1998.

Dawkins, R., *The Selfish Gene*, London: Butterworth, 1979.

Erikson, E., *Identity, Youth and Crisis*, London: Faber and Faber, 1968.

Fairbairn, R., *Collected Papers*, London: Hogarth Press, 1952.

Freud, S., 'Three Essays on Sexuality' (1905), in *Standard Edition of the Complete Psychological Works of Sigmund Freud*, Vol. 7, trans. James Strachey, London: Hogarth Press, 1953–73.

—— 'Leonardo Da Vinci' (1910), in *Standard Edition of the Complete Psychological Works of Sigmund Freud*, Vol. 9, trans. James Strachey, London: Hogarth Press, 1953–73.

—— 'On Narcissism' (1914), in *Standard Edition of the Complete Psychological Works of Sigmund Freud*, Vol. 14, trans. James Strachey, London: Hogarth Press, 1953–73.

Gabbard, G., *Psychodynamic Psychiatry in Clinical*

Practice, Washington: American Psychiatric Press, 1996.

Hamilton, V., *Narcissus and Oedipus*, London: Routledge, 1982.

Holmes, J., *The Search for the Secure Base*, London: Routledge, 2001.

Kernberg, O., *Borderline Conditions and Pathological Narcissism*, New York: New York Universities Press, 1975.

Kohut, H., *The Analysis of the Self*, New York: International Universities Press, 1971.

—— *How does Analysis Cure?* Chicago: University of Chicago Press, 1984.

Lasch, C., *The Culture of Narcissism*, New York: Doubleday, 1979.

Mollon, P., *The Fragile Self*, London: Whurr, 1993.

Morrison, A. (ed.), *Essential Papers on Narcissism*, New York: New York University Press, 1986.

Rosenfeld, H., *Psychotic States: A Psycho Analytic Approach,* New York: International Universities Press, 1965.

Spillius, E. (ed.), *Melanie Klein Today*, Vol. 1, London: Routledge, 1988.

Stern, D., *The Interpersonal World of the Infant*, New York: Basic Books, 1985.

Symmington, N., *Emotion and Spirit,* London: Karnac, 1993.

Winnicott, D., *Playing and Reality,* London: Penguin, 1971.

—— *The Maturational Processes and the Facilitating Environment*, London: Hogarth Press, 1968.